Around the World in a Flash

How the Modern World Communicates

Mark Hanlin

Canadian Edition © 2001 by Scholastic Canada Ltd.
by arrangement with Barrie Publishing Pty Limited

Around the World in a Flash

0-7791-1908-8

Text copyright © Mark Hanlin
Momentum Program © Barrie Publishing Pty Limited, 1999

Adapted for Canada by Kevin Polesello

Every effort has been made to contact the owners of the
photographs in this book. Where this has not been possible, we
invite the owners of the copyright to notify the publisher.

AP/AAP: pages 19, 37; Corel Photo Studio images 0233_039,
875081, 754059, which are protected under the copyright laws of
the U.S., Canada, and elsewhere, used under licence; International
Photographic Library: cover, 4, 5, 7, 9, 10, 15, 17, 20, 21, 24, 25,
33, 36; IPL PRO-FILE: title page, 6, 13, 22, 29; The Photo Library
– Sydney/Robert Cattan: 27; Bill Thomas: 8, 11, 12, 14, 18, 26,
28, 30, 31, 32, 34, 35.

Printed in Canada

10 9 8 7 6 5 4 3 2   03 04 05

Contents

Want to Know a Secret?

When people share their news, thoughts, and experiences with other people, it is called communication. Communication is about sending messages or passing information on to other people. Modern communications are called telecommunications. When we talk on the telephone, send an e-mail through the Internet, or are just watching television, we are using telecommunications.

Modern telecommunications use wires, optical ~~res~~, or radio and television waves to send ~~ormation~~ from one place to another – to the house ~~xt~~ door, around the world, or even into outer space. ~~e~~ information we send can be speech, computer ~~ormation~~, text, music, or pictures. This information ~~vels~~ so fast, it could circle Earth seven times per ~~ond~~.

Telecommunications have changed the way we live, ~~:~~ only in our homes, but throughout the world. The ~~:cess~~ of many businesses and industries relies on ~~dern~~ communications. They help the traffic flow in cities and help to keep food on the shelves of ~~ermarkets~~. They even help the police catch criminals.

Before telecommunications, it was more difficult stay in touch with people who lived far away. There was no way of sending a message any faster than carrying it on horseback or putting it on a train.

In the American West in 1860, Pony Express was company that ran a message service. It ran nearly 3000 kilometres from Sacramento in California to St Joseph in Missouri. Young horse-riders galloped nigh and day carrying letters and news from the other sid of the country. The riders would change horses every 15 to 20 kilometres and would average 125 kilometr per ride. Around 80 riders were needed to cover the enormous distance. The messages took up to 10 day to get to their destination.

ining All the Pieces:
he Network

ore the data or messages can travel anywhere, the
comunications must be organized into some form
network. Networks carry telephone conversations,
nputer data, and radio and television shows from
place to another. For a network to work properly, it
st know where the information is going and make
e it arrives without getting lost or damaged.

A network is similar to a road system. Sending a
ssage from one place to another on a network can
compared to travelling from one place to another in
ar. You drive down roads and turn at junctions until
get to your destination. Information travels on
es, fibre optics, or radio waves rather than roads,
turns at switches rather than junctions.

Connecting:
Who Did You Say You Wanted?

Making the right connection is essential for a communications network to run properly. With so many people wanting to communicate with each oth at the same time, you'd think that the connections could get easily mixed up. How do calls stay on the right track so you don't end up talking to a fast-food restaurant instead of your best friend?

All the telephone lines in a town or region are connected to an exchange. Each exchange is programmed to know which telephone line goes wit which telephone number.

When you dial a number on a telephone, the number code is sent through telephone lines until it arrives at the exchange. The exchange reads the cod number and connects your line to the number you want. It also sends an electrical charge down the lin to make the oth person's teleph ring. When they pick up the receiver, a switc in the phone tu the ringer off ar you're connecte

8

When the telephone system first began, exchanges used people to switch calls. A person making a call didn't dial a number but picked up the telephone and talked to a human operator. The operators would switch calls by plugging one line into another – a bit like putting an electric plug into a socket. This was called a manual exchange. As more and more people had telephones installed, the exchanges grew bigger. Some large exchanges had hundreds of operators switching calls by hand.

Modern telephone exchanges can automatically connect hundreds or even thousands of calls at once. These exchanges are all connected together to form a large telephone network. A network is much more efficient, using many smaller exchanges instead of one big one. It is less expensive and makes all the connections easier to manage.

If you are dialling someone who is not connected to your local exchange, the exchange will switch your call to the next town or region's exchange. The farther away the telephone you are calling, the more switches the exchanges have to make

A videoconference enables people to see each other as they communicate.

A telephone call travelling across the country might have to go through many switches to reach its destination. Modern telephone exchanges are getting smarter, too. If too many calls are going through one exchange, they can divert to another exchange and find their way around the traffic jam.

The most advanced telephone exchanges allow three or more callers to connect to the same line at once. Business people call it a conference line.

Look, No Cables!

A radio telephone.

Modern communications systems enable people to live in very remote areas of the world. Some live on islands and in lighthouses. Others live in deserts or on farms where the nearest neighbour is a few hundred kilometres away. For many of these people, communication is very important. It is their only connection with the outside world. But there is a problem.

Installing telephone cables to these distant areas is too expensive, considering the small number of people that would be using the service. To provide at least telephone communications, many of these distant areas are connected to the network using radio. Radio networks connect police, ambulance, and many other services. They connect ships at sea and even emergency telephones on highways.

Radio communication doesn't require cables because it works on a system of electric waves that travel through the air. The waves are sent by a transmitter and are received at the other end by a receiver. Radio waves travel through the air in different lengths. Some are long waves, others are short. A special little electronic device called a tuner can pick out a particular length of these waves and send them to the radio. Each wavelength corresponds to a particular frequency. Radio waves have hundreds of thousands of frequencies.

Using different frequencies allows many people to communicate using radio. It allows people to use cell phones at the same time without interfering with each other's calls. It ensures that police radio messages don't get mixed up with firefighters' or pilots' radio communications messages.

This tower transmits radio waves.

Hey! Where Are You?

Cell phones also communicate using radio waves. They are very popular because they can be used almost anywhere in the country. People like to know they can be contacted wherever they travel.

To make the cell-phone system work properly, transmitting and receiving stations have been installed at regular intervals all around the country. The areas that these stations cover are called cells. This is why the cell-phone system is referred to as a cellular network. If the cell phone moves away from one cell and the radio signal becomes weak, the system automatically switches to another cell closer to the phone. This means people can travel great distances without having their calls interrupted.

Television

Radio waves are also used to send television pictures and sound into our homes and offices. These signals also use different frequencies that we commonly refer to as channels. Since television was introduced, it has changed our lives. It can entertain us, educate us, and bring us up to date with news from around the world.

Television is also delivered by cable into many of our homes. Cable television can carry many more channels than television sent over the air. A television signal uses a lot more information than the telephone network could carry. That's why television has its own broadcast and cable networks. These networks are specially designed to carry television programs all over the country and all over the world.

A new system of television has been developed called High-Definition Television or HDTV. This system offers much sharper, clearer pictures than our present television system. This will be particularly good for people who like large television screens.

Satellites

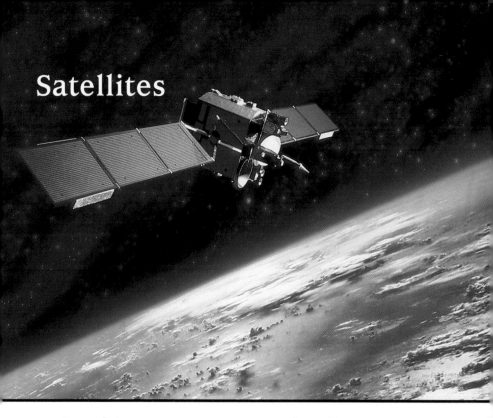

One of the most common ways of sending television pictures, computer data, and telephone calls over long distances is via a communications satellite. When communications have to travel overseas or across countries, normal radio waves aren't strong enough to travel the great distances. This is because buildings and mountains between the transmitter and receiver quickly weaken the signal.

Satellites are launched into space using a rocket or a space shuttle. They travel close to 30 000 kilometres per hour or more just to stay in orbit around Earth. Communications satellites are about the size of a car or a bus. Their electronic circuits are powered by large solar panels that convert sunlight into electricity.

Many of the homes in this neighbourhood have satellite dishes.

A communications satellite is so high in the sky that the signal travels straight up from Earth without any interference at all. The signals are received by the satellite in space and then retransmitted back to a receiving station on Earth. Sometimes, if a signal needs to travel farther, it will be received on Earth and sent back up to another satellite. Some satellites can even send signals to each other before retransmitting them back to Earth. This means satellites can send signals anywhere in the world.

Satellites don't just send their signal down to one spot. A satellite can transmit to a special area called a footprint. The area that a footprint covers is determined by the people who own the satellite. These footprints can be enormous areas the size of a whole continent, or they can be much smaller. Footprints are often used when satellites send television programs directly to people's homes via a small satellite-receiving dish on roofs.

Satellites orbit Earth at different heights and speeds depending on the job they have to do. Many communications satellites orbit at the same speed that Earth is spinning. This means that the satellite always stays in the same spot above Earth. If you could see the satellite in the sky, it would appear not to be moving. These satellites are used for telecommunications because they can transmit to one area continuously without moving. These "geostationary satellites" sit 35 600 kilometres above Earth. The problem with these satellites is that, because they are so far away from Earth, the signals take a quarter of a second to travel through space. This can create an echo for people talking on the telephone and can also cause irritating delays. New systems of lower-orbit satellites are solving those time delay problems.

Satellite Phones

In the late 1990s, a new cell phone system called Iridium was introduced. Although they are not much bigger than normal cell phones, Iridium phones connect directly to a network of 66 lower-orbit satellites around Earth. This means that people can use this phone anywhere in the world while keeping the same phone number. The system isn't perfect – satellite phones don't work indoors yet. To make them work properly, you have to be outdoors with a clear view of the sky.

Help! Where Am I?

Another network of satellites orbiting Earth is called the Global Positioning System or GPS. This network of 24 satellites allows people with a special receiver to work out where they are anywhere on Earth to within a few metres. This technology was originally developed for use by the United States Armed Forces, but now anyone can use it. The receiving units are cheap to buy and very portable.

GPS has many uses. Ships and airplanes can find their way using GPS as a navigation tool. If they get into trouble, they can radio the rescue authorities their exact position. Taxi and transport companies can monitor the exact position of all their vehicles so they can provide a better service.

Car drivers can also use GPS. Using a special navigation system, drivers can not only find their location, but can be offered directions by their car's

on-board computer. In Japan, over 500 000 vehicles have already been fitted with a navigation system that uses GPS.

Move Over!

Although satellites have revolutionized telecommunications, they do have their limitations. Satellites only last a few years before they have to be replaced. This is very expensive and occasionally unreliable. Rockets launching the satellites into space can sometimes explode. Even when satellites make it into orbit, there is still a danger that they could break down or be damaged by passing space junk.

A cheaper, more reliable carrier is emerging to ease the increasing load on the telecommunications network. This carrier doesn't use wires or radio waves or even cables. It is made of tiny glass tubes no thicker than a human hair. The information travels down these tiny tubes as pulses of light. These tubes are called fibre optics.

The Big Pipes: Fibre Optics

Fibre optics were first introduced in the 1980s after years of testing. An intense laser beam of light travels through the centre of the glass fibre by reflecting down the fibre walls like a mirror. All the information is contained in the light beam. It might sound a bit like science fiction, but it's true.

Digital information is information that is expressed in the form of two numbers – one and zero. Computers and telecommunications systems send these ones and zeros in a particular order to communicate and send information. They send these numbers using electricity. When this information reaches a fibre-optic cable, the numbers must be converted into a light beam before they can travel through the cable.

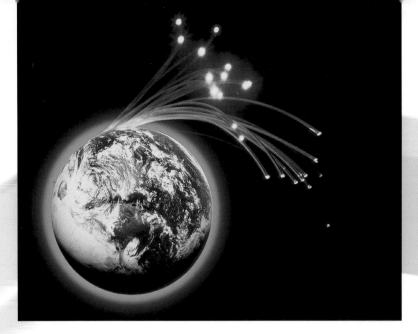

The light beam is broken up into bursts or pulses of light. There are only two types of pulse – big pulses and little pulses. These pulses represent the digital information or data. Once the light pulses travel along the fibre and reach the other end, they must be converted back into electrical digital information.

Fibre-optic cables can carry telephone calls, computer data, sound, and moving pictures at an incredible speed – faster than any other type of carrier. They were first used to link cities' telephone exchanges together. A fibre-optic cable is not just one hair-like fibre, but hundreds of them bunched together. The first cable was able to support more than 40 000 telephone conversations taking place at the same time. Using new technology, cables are being designed to carry around 500 000 calls at the same time – that's the equivalent of sending 90 000 volumes of an encyclopedia around the world in just one second!

Undersea Cables

These days, fibre optics is being used in undersea cables that link communication centres around the world. The enormous capacity of fibre optics makes these cables a more reliable and often more affordable alternative to satellites.

Waterproof cables, laid underneath the sea, have made telecommunications possible between continents and cities for over a hundred years. The cables are laid using a special boat that rolls the cable out from a big drum. Undersea cables link major cities all over the world. Fibre-optic cables have been laid under the sea since 1988.

One day, when it becomes less expensive, people's houses may be linked to the network with a tiny hair-like fibre optic. Most of this enormous carrying capacity won't be used for phone calls. It will support the newest and biggest information revolution of our time – the Internet.

Surfing the Net

The Internet is another communications network that links computers. The Internet uses telephone lines or cable or satellite systems to connect computers all over the world. The system is vast and complex, like a gigantic spider web. That is why it is also called the World Wide Web.

By linking computers, people can share information and send each other messages. When people are looking for information on the Internet or just having fun, they are often referred to as "surfing the Net."

Most information from the Internet arrives on your computer screen as pages called Websites. Each Website contains pages with text, pictures, or links to speech, sounds, music, and television. Looking for anything on the Internet usually requires you to find Websites using a search engine. You type in a word, and a very powerful computer will search through the millions of Web pages available on the Internet. The results will come up as Web pages containing the word you have typed in.

Connecting

When we dial a telephone, we reach an exchange that connects our call. When we connect to the Internet, our computer dials the phone and connects to an Internet Service Provider or ISP. An ISP is the equivalent of a telephone exchange. It connects your computer to the World Wide Web of computer addresses through the telephone system.

Computers can also connect to an ISP using satellite systems or the cable lines used to carry TV signals.

You can connect to your ISP using a special device called a modem. A modem connects your computer to the ISP by converting your computer's signals into signals that can travel up and down telephone or cable lines.

An ISP might have thousands of computers connected to its service. Besides being used by people at home, these computers could be used by people in businesses, government or education departments, and other organizations.

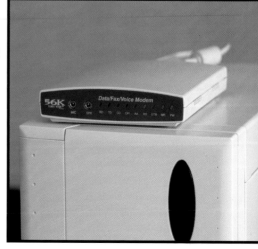

A modem connects your computer to the World Wide Web via an ISP. Many new computers come with built-in modems.

Where Are All the Websites?

If people want to put information on the Web, they can use a program on their computer to make the Web pages. They transfer the Web pages from their computer to the ISP's computer through the modem. Each person or organization has an amount of space on their ISP's computer for a Website. Every Website has a special computer address called an URL. When other people look up Websites, the pages they visit are on the ISP's computer, not the people's personal or office computers.

www dot

Since the introduction of the World Wide Web in the early 1990s, the Internet has become much easier to use. This is mainly due to a program that was developed to link Web pages together so information was easy to follow. Using a computer mouse, people can click on pictures or text that will take them to another page or another Website of information. Every Web page in the world has a different computer address. When you click on a link, it tells the computer the new address to go to.

When you read a Web page, it might have links to other subjects you like. All you have to do is click on the subject and the computer switches to that next Website. It might not be just words and pictures either – it could be a music or television program.

Besides using it for looking up information, the Internet can be a lot of fun. Linking computers together in a network means people can play computer games against each other. If everyone is running the same program, you can be in a car race against drivers from all over the world.

Cyberspace Cafés

You can write letters on a computer and send them to other people who are connected to the Internet. This is called e-mail, which is short for "electronic mail." Unlike normal mail, e-mail arrives almost instantaneously at its destination, which could be anywhere in the world. You can send many messages simultaneously via e-mail, for a fraction of the cost of an international phone call.

People can communicate on the Internet in other ways besides sending e-mail. Videoconferences have been used by businesses for some years, but they run on a different system from the Internet and are very expensive. Now people from around the world can meet each other using a special program, a camera, and a microphone plugged into their computer. Not only can you talk to people, you can see them as well.

People can get together by going to a certain Internet address and viewing a list of other people who are available to talk. If you click on a name, and that person wants to talk to you, you're connected. With some programs, you can have even 10 other people connected at the same time.

If you don't have a camera or a microphone, you can still talk to other people by typing messages and posting them in a "chat room." Chat and videoconference rooms also have special-interest rooms. This means that if you are interested in a certain subject, you can find a place to talk with a group of people sharing the same interest.

The Internet is just one of many computer networks. Businesses often link all their computers in an office to share information. Banks use networks to connect their automatic bank machines and credit card facilities to the bank's main computers.

The World Wide Wait

Despite the amazing things the Internet can do, many people complain that it is slow and sometimes doesn't even work. The Internet was never designed to handle the massive amount of information people would like to send through it. That's why Internet television doesn't look very good and why pages and pictures can sometimes take very long to appear on the screen. Many people believe a major overhaul of the network is needed before good-quality television and CD-quality music can be sent properly.

People also complain that finding something they want isn't always easy. The problem is that because the network is connected up to so many millions of Web pages, searching through a particular subject can take hours. There is often too much information about a subject, and most of it isn't what you want.

People are redesigning the search engines that find the information on the Internet so that searching will become easier. In the future, you might be able to tell a special search engine what specific information you need and why you need it. The program would search the Internet and make more decisions about what information was important and what was not. While it was searching and sifting through the information, you could be doing other things. An example could be a search for information on airplanes. Telling a search engine to find out how an airplane works for a school project you are doing could greatly limit the answers you get back. You wouldn't have to waste your time looking through the sites that sell airplanes, airplane parts, flights, or tours. The computer could do that.

This is starting to happen. There are special Websites you can visit and customize to your own tastes. This means that you can program the Website to bring you news, events, and other information you might be interested in. When you first visit the site, it asks you questions about yourself: your likes and dislikes, where you live, how old you are. It gives you a special code name and password so that when you visit the site again, the Web page is customized for you. This page can have, for example, the news and weather in your local area and current news and information that might interest you.

Wearing the Internet in the Future

The Internet is becoming more and more like a one-stop shop. You can buy things, play games, go to the bank, learn, watch television, or talk to others all from the one spot – your computer. At the moment, most computers stay in one place. There are portable computers and laptop computers, but you still have to set them up to use them.

People are designing computers so that you can carry them around with you, even wear them in your clothing. One particular vision of the future could see everyone wearing computers, so that they became part of you.

You wouldn't need a keyboard because you could talk to the computer instead. These computers would also be connected to the Internet all the time, similar to the way cell phones are connected to a network now. The computer wouldn't be just a computer as we know it today. It would be a telephone, videophone, fax machine, radio, television, and much more – all your telecommunications in one package. You could see the people you were talking to, or see information you had found, on a screen in front of your eyes. This screen could be built into a pair of glasses or even be a thin layer of plastic that covers your eyes like contact lenses. If you wanted to have fun, you could play a game by yourself or with some friends over the network.

The Future: I Want It Now

The world's first image-transmitting cellular phone with a digital camera.

Even if we're not wearing computers for a few years, the way we communicate is certainly changing. The Internet, television, and telephones may merge together to become one communication unit that you carry around with you. Although it is very hard to predict exactly the way future telecommunications will go, there are some indications.

The cell-phone network will get better and cheaper to use. When cell-phone calls are very cheap, people will be able to access more information with them more often.

The new generation of cell phones may have television screens that allow people to watch video clips. Instead of using a keypad for dialling and giving instructions, people will use their voices to tell their phones what to do. Already there are phones that can dial a person's number when you say a name. Telephones of the future will be called communications devices.

Regardless of the amazing innovations in telecommunications, people should remember not to get lost in cyberspace and not to talk to and be entertained solely by machines. Let's hope that there will always be time to put our communication devices away and talk to the person beside us.

Glossary

convert   to change or transform

customize   to build, fit, or alter something to suit an individual's needs

destination   a place at the end of a journey

exchange   a central telephone office where connections are made

junction   a point where two or more things are joined

modem   from modulator/demodulator, a device that receives and sends signals along telephone or cable lines

orbit   to move or travel on a curved or circular path

pulse   a single signal

remote   far away from the main centres of population

simultaneously   at the same time

URL   universal resource locator, Website address

videophone   a telephone that sends a picture or video as well as sound so the users can see each other

Index